TEN MARKS AND A TRAIN TICKET

Benno's Escape to Freedom

by Susy Goldstein, Gina Hamilton
and Wendy Share

Holocaust & Hope Testimonial Series: Children of the Kindertransport

League for
Human Rights of
B'nai Brith
Canada
Ligue
des droits
de la
personne

THE LEAGUE FOR HUMAN RIGHTS OF B'NAI BRITH CANADA

Photo of train tracks in Auschwitz Memorial on the cover and Israeli flag on page 111 © BigStockPhoto. Historical photos on pages 16, 18, 20–23, 36, 48, 54, 55, 59, 62, 63, 65, 70, 71, 73, 74, 80, 82, 96, and 110–111 (historical timeline photos) provided by the Wiener Library.

LIBRARY AND ARCHIVES CANADA CATALOGUING IN PUBLICATION
Ten marks and a train ticket: Benno's escape to freedom /
Susy Goldstein, Gina Hamilton, Wendy Share.

ISBN 978-0-9784174-0-6

1. Kindertransports (Rescue operations)—Juvenile literature.
2. World War, 1939–1945—Jews—Rescue—Juvenile literature. 3. World War, 1939–1945—Children—Juvenile literature. 4. Refugee children—Biography—Juvenile literature. 5. Refugees, Jewish—Biography—Juvenile literature.
I. Share, Wendy, 1961– II. Hamilton, Gina, 1957– III. Goldstein, Susy, 1955–
IV. League for Human Rights of B'nai Brith Canada V. Title.

DS135.E6H359 2007   j940.53′18350922   C2007-905159-6

Published by the League for Human Rights of B'nai Brith Canada
15 Hove Street, Toronto, Ontario M3H 4Y8
E-mail: league@bnaibrith.ca | Website: www.bnaibrith.ca
For more information about this book, visit www.holocaustandhope.ca
Third printing | Printed in Canada

CALLAWIND
CHILDREN'S BOOKS
Produced by Callawind Children's Books
A division of Callawind Publications Inc.
3551 St. Charles Boulevard, Suite 179, Kirkland, Quebec H9H 3C4
E-mail: info@callawind.com | Website: www.callawind.com
Design: Marcy Claman

TEN MARKS AND A TRAIN TICKET

Benno's Escape to Freedom

In memory of Charlie and the other

1,500,000 Jewish children who were murdered

in the Holocaust.

~

This book is dedicated to our children,

and our children's children.

PREFACE

THE PUBLICATION OF *Ten Marks and a Train Ticket*, the first in the League for Human Rights' *Holocaust and Hope Testimonial Series*, marks the culmination of decades of Holocaust education undertaken by the League throughout Canadian society. The League, dedicated to combating anti-Semitism and bigotry wherever it strikes, has a proud history of pioneering the first *Holocaust and Hope* study tours for educators to Germany, Poland and Israel more than two decades ago. Its team of dedicated experts works closely with teachers to develop Holocaust curricula in the context of anti-racist education in Canada.

As our concept of a *Holocaust and Hope Testimonial Series* developed, with its goal of highlighting the experiences of Canadians who were child survivors of the Holocaust, we were fortunate to meet Susy Goldstein, Gina Hamilton and Wendy Share, the authors of this important historical record. We are grateful to them for sharing with us—and now with you—the narrative of their father's escape to freedom, a child of the *Kindertransport*.

Benno was one of 9,600 children who were safely evacuated to England on the *Kindertransport* (children's transport). The Jewish Refugee Committee persuaded the British Government to let in a maximum of 10,000 unaccompanied children under the age of 18 from Germany, Austria and Czechoslovakia. The children of the *Kindertransport,* unlike the vast majority of Jewish children across Eastern Europe, ultimately survived, going on to thrive in their adopted countries. Canada would later become Benno's new home.

We felt that Benno's inspirational journey would be an appropriate beginning to our *Series,* allowing students to learn about the Holocaust from Benno's own experiences. They will learn of the tortuous choices faced by Jewish families who tried to send their children to safety. Alas, of the 6,000,000 Jews murdered by the Nazis, 1,500,000 were children.

Benno's testimonial should not stand solely as an event in history that occurred in another place at another time. Our goal must be to ensure that the unique lessons of the Holocaust are never forgotten. From Benno's story, we must learn the dangers of staying silent when confronted by anti-Semitism, racism or bigotry of any kind.

The League is proud to present to you *Ten Marks and a Train Ticket,* the story of a Canadian with a personal history that reaches out to touch all our hearts.

Professor Alain Goldschläger
Ontario Chair
League for Human Rights
Director, Holocaust Research Institute
University of Western Ontario

L. Ruth Klein
National Director
League for Human Rights
Editor-in-Chief, Holocaust
& Hope Testimonial Series

INTRODUCTION

AFTER THE ATTACKS OF SEPTEMBER 11, 2001, we felt that it was important to tell our father's story. We could no longer stand by silently and let evil destroy innocent families as it had during World War II. Growing up, we knew that our father had escaped from Berlin, Germany, because of the Nazi onslaught against the Jews. However, he rarely talked in detail about his experiences. We began asking him questions, and to our surprise he showed us the book he had written over 60 years before, when he was 16 years old. It told the story of his escape from Nazi Germany on the *Kindertransport*. To retell our father's story, we relied on his amazing memory, on his book that he had saved for so many years, and on family photos and documents.

We strongly believe we must pass on our father's story to ensure that both the hatred and the kindness of others will never be forgotten, and that vital lessons will be learned from history. The most important lesson of his experience is that bigotry does not simply end with the persecution of innocent people, but can lead to mass murder. This is the breaking point that finally pushes bystanders into action, but such help often comes too late and benefits too few. We believe that the more people know about our father's story, the less willing they will be to stand by and let atrocities like the Holocaust happen again.

We would like to thank the following people who provided us with guidance in the writing of this book, first and foremost our parents. Without their guidance, discussion and review, this book would not have been written. Our father's keen desire for accuracy has been our guiding principle. Second, we would like to thank Ruth Klein, Anita Bromberg, Karen Lazar, and Sol Israel of the League for Human Rights of B'nai Brith Canada, who had the vision and commitment to help us bring this project to completion. Also, members of the League for Human Rights' Holocaust Education Committee chaired by Professor Alain Goldschläger: Professor Lennox Borel, Stella Watson, Leon Lenchner and Sabrina Gallo. Without their time and dedication to this project and their thoughtful input, we would not have made it. Third, we would like to thank Marcy Claman for her assistance, as well as everyone who helped us with the editing process. We would also like to thank our donors for believing in the importance of bringing this true story to light. Lastly, we would like to thank our families for their support and encouragement.

PROLOGUE

MOST PEOPLE WILL REMEMBER September 11, 2001, for the terrible destruction of the World Trade Center in New York City. For me, it is the day that confirmed that my parents and little brother were murdered by the Nazis in Auschwitz, a concentration camp in Poland.

While most of the world watched terror unfold on their television screens, I stood at the entrance to the Jewish Museum in Berlin, Germany. My wife and I walked upstairs into the first room of the museum. I did not know what to expect. For the very first time I saw definite proof that my parents, Max and Golda, and my younger brother, Charlie, then just seven years of age, had been killed in Auschwitz in June 1943. I had been searching my whole life for this proof.

Until today, I had kept alive some hope that maybe, somehow, they had survived the Nazi atrocities. I still have not given up hope that somewhere, sometime, I might still find a surviving family member. I will never give up hope and I will never stop searching.

This is my story. *Bruno*

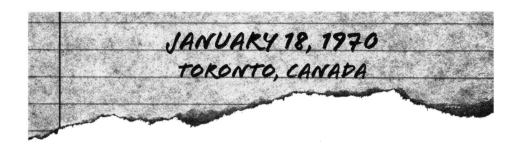

MY DAUGHTER TURNS NINE TODAY. We all sit around the dining room table for Friday night dinner. I know that tonight is the night I must tell my story. I take a deep breath as I pause to gather my thoughts. I was a boy of nine when my parents sent me away. How can a child of nine understand why parents would ever send their own children away?

My wife, Rita, starts to light the *Shabbat* candles. As we begin to eat the *challah* and chicken soup, I turn to my daughter and say, "I have something to talk to you all about tonight. This is not easy for me to discuss, but, in January 1939, I was sitting at the dinner table with my parents and brothers exactly like we are tonight. My parents told us that my brother and I were to leave our home in Berlin on our own within the next few days. Can you imagine if this were the last Friday night we were to be together as a family?"

IT WAS FRIDAY NIGHT. I remember it clearly. In my mind I can see us all sitting around the dining room table. My father, Max, sits down at the head of the table. Golda, my mother, starts lighting the *Shabbat* candles. My little brother, Charlie, who is not quite three, sits beside me. He is kicking my

Golda, Charlie, Heinz, Max, Benno
(left to right) in 1937

leg under the table. My older brother, Heinz, sits opposite my mother. As we begin to eat the *challah* and chicken soup, my father says, "I have something important to say tonight. This is very difficult for us, but your mother and I have decided that the two of you, Heinz and Benno, will leave Berlin in the next few days. It's not safe here anymore for us Jews. We will follow as soon as we can."

This was the last Friday night dinner we were together as a family.

1933–1939
BERLIN, GERMANY

IN 1933, PRESIDENT PAUL VON HINDENBURG appointed Adolf Hitler as Chancellor of Germany. Shortly after this appointment, Hindenburg died and Hitler took over the presidency as well. At that time, more than 62,000,000 people lived in Germany. Only 500,000 were Jews, less than 1% of the population.

When Hitler came to power, more than 5,500,000 people in Germany were out of work. Hitler and his Nazi party accused the Jews of causing this unemployment. Before long, large numbers of unemployed Germans backed him. Hitler, known as the *Führer,* took on the powers of a dictator and began taking action against Germany's Jews. In 1935, Hitler passed the first of the Nuremberg Laws, taking German citizenship away from Jews. The Nazis also began sending Jews to concentration camps where they were brutalized and murdered. By 1936, Jews were not allowed to vote. Signs reading "Jews Not Welcome" appeared in many German cities.

Life was becoming harder and harder for Jews in Germany. Families that could obtain visas left right away. Others could not get visas, or stayed because they thought that things could not possibly get any worse.

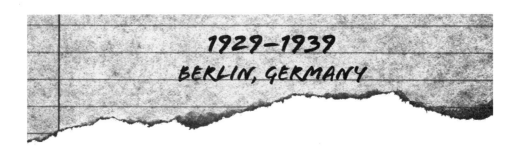

1929–1939
BERLIN, GERMANY

I WAS BORN ON AUGUST 6, 1929. Until January 1939, I lived with my parents and brothers in Berlin, Germany. We were a happy family and I was especially close to my mother. I remember often spending time with her in the kitchen as she prepared dinner for us.

We lived in a large, multi-level apartment house on *Fehrbelliner Strasse*, in the north of Berlin. My grandmother, Frimke, lived in the apartment above us. We would visit back and forth with her all the time.

Grandmother Frimke

My father had his own tailor shop at the front of the building. He designed, cut and hand-sewed suits. I loved watching him work in the shop, and examined all the different bolts of cloth he had on the shelves. I often watched him working with a tape measure around his neck and a pin in his mouth. He used his big heavy iron to press the suits he made for his customers. I

Max and Golda in 1936 with Baby Charlie
in front of their tailor shop

remember playing with samples of fabric that he gave us after a season was over. One season, however, I remember cutting up the samples of fabric for the new season instead! He wasn't very pleased with me that day.

I went to a Jewish school not far from our house. I really liked school. I had a lot of friends and I studied hard in my classes. The street next to ours was very steep. Often on our way home from school, I would stand at the top of the street and try and guess the type of car driving up the hill before we saw it. Most of the cars were Mercedes or Opels and we had to guess the model. I was very good at this game. On weekends, I played soccer on the street

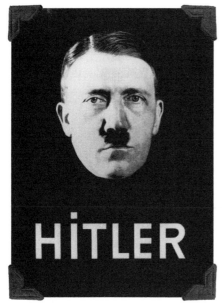

A 1932 election poster   *Nazi Party rally, 1934*

in front of my father's shop with my brother and all of our friends. We were like any other German Jewish family of that time.

When Hitler was elected leader, one of his first important changes was the passing of the Nuremburg Laws. Life started to change for us almost immediately. The new laws discouraged non-Jews from shopping at Jewish businesses, which meant my father had fewer customers. Money became tight for us and my mother was very careful when she went shopping for food.

Pictures of Hitler were now everywhere: in public schools, shops, offices, and even in private houses. Soon, more and more men in brown and black Nazi uniforms with swastika armbands appeared on

*Heinz (2nd from the left, middle row) in a class photo
at his Jewish school in 1938*

the streets. It was common to see them as we walked to school. My brother and I would often stop talking and walk with our eyes straight ahead as we passed the Nazis. The swastika started appearing on stamps and flags, too. Every non-Jewish house was now supposed to have a flag, so since we didn't have one, everyone knew we were Jews.

The government banned Jewish schools and organizations, and so our school was closed. Luckily, there was a Jewish school around the corner that was overlooked by the Nazis and my parents sent us there, but this was only a temporary arrangement and I wasn't as happy. In 1938, the Nazis announced that Jews were forbidden to play outside. This was very hard for us as we loved playing outdoors. I used to enjoy going to the movies, but the Nazis put a stop to that as well. There were now notices posted outside all swimming pools, movie theatres, skating rinks and other places: No Jews Allowed.

Still, my family remained close and tried to live a normal life. We ate dinner together every night. On Saturdays, we went to synagogue. Our apartment was filled with friends and relatives for the Jewish holidays.

Humiliation of two Jewish school boys in front of their classmates

I never realized why Papa was so worried and why he and Mama were always whispering. They must have tried very hard not to let us know how scared they were. We didn't have much money and knew not to waste food, but we did spend money on postage stamps. In desperation, my parents sent many letters to relatives in the United States, hoping that they could help us get a visa and find us a new home where we could be safe.

NOVEMBER 9 AND 10, 1938
BERLIN, GERMANY

ON NOVEMBER 9, 1938, Nazi storm troopers and members of the SS and Hitler Youth attacked and murdered Jews, broke into and wrecked Jewish homes, and brutalized Jewish men, women and children. All over Germany and Austria, the windows of Jewish shops were smashed, and everything inside destroyed. Synagogues and sacred *Torah* scrolls were set on fire. Local firefighters stood and watched, or simply kept the fires from spreading to surrounding buildings. They did not even try to put them out.

In total, 267 synagogues and 7,500 Jewish shops were destroyed, and over 100 Jews were killed. About 25,000 men were rounded up and sent to concentration camps. Many of the Jews were tortured, and in some cases randomly beaten to death.

This terrible event became known as *Kristallnacht,* Night of the Broken Glass, because the next day the streets were covered in pieces of glass from all the broken windows. Three days later, the top Nazi leaders met to assess the damage of November 9 and 10. They decided that it was the Jews themselves who were responsible for *Kristallnacht,* and fined them 1,000,000 marks for the damage.

AROUND 8 P.M. ON NOVEMBER 9, a group of men in Nazi uniforms appeared on our street. They began marching, stopping at all Jewish shops, homes and synagogues in the area. A massive attack was underway. In a brutal night of chaos, the Nazis destroyed everything in their path that could be identified as Jewish. They pulled the shutters off my father's tailor shop and shattered the windows. They threw cloth and half-made garments onto the floor, and smashed the large worktable. They looted my parents' bedroom, which was immediately

Mother and child passing by smashed shop windows after Kristallnacht

Destroyed Jewish shop in Berlin after Kristallnacht

behind the shop, overturning the large dresser and breaking the mirror. They destroyed our synagogue, along with many others. We watched in horror that terrible night as soldiers took my father away to Dachau concentration camp, where he was detained for six weeks, and then released.

My brother, Heinz, turned 13 on November 24, but because my father was in the concentration camp and because of all the destruction and terror, his *bar mitzvah* was cancelled. He never got a chance to read from the *Torah*, or celebrate with the Jewish community.

When my father returned from Dachau, the whispering between Papa and Mama increased. My brothers and I didn't know what was going on, but we could feel something awful in the air. We had to leave Germany and escape Nazi rule. Our parents' fears for our safety had intensified.

FOR MANY MONTHS, OUR WHOLE FAMILY prepared to leave Berlin. My parents had sold some of our furniture to pay for train tickets and wrote letters to try to get visas. We planned to leave together and go to our relatives in the United States, but the proper documents never arrived.

After *Kristallnacht*, life was very unsafe for Jewish children in Berlin. I could often hear Hitler Youth laugh and shout "Kill the Jews" as I walked

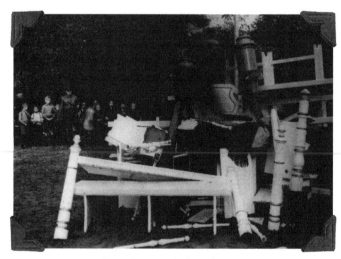

Synagogue furnishings piled up for public burning during Kristallnacht

home. I dreaded the end of the school day and would run as fast as I could to get away from the name-calling and threats. I had already come home with a bruised face and a black eye. While walking through the streets, I was constantly scared that someone would throw a stone at me or beat me.

A few days after *Kristallnacht,* Mama asked me to take my brother, Charlie, for a walk. As I pushed his stroller around the block, a group of Hitler Youth attacked us. They set a dog on me, and it tried to bite my leg. I was terrified. I pushed Charlie's stroller home as fast as I could, with the Hitler Youth charging after us. As we reached the corner of our street, I saw a painter on a very high ladder painting window frames. The Hitler Youth forgot about Charlie and me, and started calling the painter names and shaking the ladder. All of a

Adolf Hitler with members of the Hitler Youth in 1938

sudden, he fell to the ground and was killed right before my eyes. I can't describe how afraid I was. I had never imagined anyone could do such a thing, and I got Charlie home as quickly as I could. I could barely tell Mama the story through my sobs. It was after this incident that my parents realized just how unsafe Berlin had become.

Golda and Max

It wasn't unusual for me to play with a friend one day, and then hear the next that he and his family had left in the night. Our friends probably didn't even know they were leaving. Their families left as quietly as possible, hoping that the Nazis wouldn't catch them.

Weeks passed and we didn't get our visas. I think it was during this time that my parents felt they had no choice but to send their children away to safety as soon as they could.

The Escape Route from Germany

During that Friday night dinner in January, my parents outlined their simple escape plan to us. They had made it quickly, not really knowing the conditions outside Germany. At first they were going to send us to Belgium. Then they learned of two boys down the street who were caught trying to enter Belgium and hadn't been heard from since.

Mama and Papa had heard that the Jewish Refugee Committee in Holland was watching for children arriving illegally and had sent people to the train stations and border crossings to help them. My parents had also heard that the Germans would allow children out of the country without passports. The hardest thing would be to get past the border guards into Holland. Normally, you need a passport to enter another country and we didn't have such a document. In spite of these risks, our parents decided to send us to Holland.

I couldn't believe what I was hearing, Papa expected my brother and me to leave by ourselves. The two of us had never done anything on our own before. We were going on a train, all alone, with no one to tell us what to do. "We're going to have a new experience," I thought at first. Little did I realize how much this train ride would change my life, or that it would take me away from the family I loved so much.

Heinz got very quiet and I'm sure he must have been very scared. I think he understood a little bit more about what was happening than I did. After all, he was already 13 years old, and I imagine he knew some of the dangers we faced.

As I lay in bed that night, I thought about the next morning. I tossed and turned as I tried to imagine a life without my parents and little brother. Charlie and I shared a bedroom. He was still a little boy, but we had become close over the last few months. I was going to miss him a lot.

I was thinking about what I should bring on our journey when my eyes closed and I drifted off to sleep.

Heinz, Golda, Benno, Max (left to right) in 1935

JANUARY 29, 1939
BERLIN, GERMANY

THE NEXT MORNING, I woke up and reluctantly got out of bed. I dressed quickly and went to see what my parents had prepared for our journey. Mama had breakfast on the table and Papa and Heinz were already sitting down. No-one said a word. I guess we were all thinking our own private thoughts. I ate my breakfast slowly, hoping to delay leaving home.

On the floor in the kitchen was a large, brown leather suitcase with clothes, photographs of Mama, Papa and Charlie, toys, and books. Two brown, tweed knickerbocker suits, which my father had just finished making for us, were hanging on the door. The material was very thick and bulky.

"These are for you," my father said to us. I immediately tried mine on. It fit perfectly. I felt very proud of my new suit; I thought I looked a lot older than nine. I put a few more books into the suitcase, which was packed right to the top with all our treasured possessions. We had to sit on it to close it.

Papa turned to Heinz. "Benno is only nine years old. He needs you to look after him. I want you to remember something. Do not come back to Berlin. Whatever happens, it is not safe here for Jews. We will follow you as soon as we can."

Mama, who had been standing and watching us all quietly, started to cry. Watching the tears roll down her cheeks made me so sad, and I wanted to run to her. My father looked at her and said, "Come now, Golda, don't let the boys see you so unhappy. They might not want to leave if you seem so sad. You know it's for the best. We must let them have their chance at life."

Max

Golda

For many years, when I thought about being sent away I became very upset. As a teenager, I remember being very annoyed at my parents. I thought that they hadn't really loved us at all. They had just tried to get rid of us. How can parents who love you one day just send you away into the unknown? I couldn't understand what they had done. But as I became an adult with children of my own, I began to realize that theirs was the supreme act of kindness and selflessness.

As we got ready to leave for the train station, my father gave us some advice. "If you are turned back from the border, follow the guard's orders. But at the first chance you get, when the train stops, get off and try again. Hide on the train if you have to, but get out of Germany any way you can. Once you are out of Germany, you will be safe. Try to find the Jewish Refugee Committee. They will give you food and somewhere to sleep. We will come and meet you as soon as we can."

Then my father gave us each our own birth certificate. "Put it in a safe place, Benno. I couldn't get you a passport. This is the only document you will have for the journey and the border guards." I put the birth certificate in the inside of my coat in a small hidden pocket. My father then handed each of us 10 marks (the equivalent of $100.00 today). "I can only give each of you 10 marks. That is all that is allowed," my father said. "It's too big a risk to hide more money than that on you." My father also gave me a pocket watch and a pen, probably to encourage me to write as much as possible. A few days before leaving, I had gone with my mother to buy them for the journey.

I remember how I walked into my bedroom one last time. Now Charlie would have the bedroom all to himself. "I sure hope it won't be too long before

Charlie in 1938

all five of us are together again," I thought.

I wasn't very happy at the thought of just my brother and me on a long train ride. I did not realize the extent of the nightmare that we were about to undertake in our efforts to escape.

JANUARY 29, 1939
LEAVING BERLIN, GERMANY

WALKING DOWN MY STREET FOR THE LAST TIME, I saw lots of destruction and wreckage. We passed SS guards on the way. Many of the shops had been boarded up, and terrible anti-Semitic graffiti was scrawled everywhere. In the distance I saw the milkman making his early morning deliveries. Across the way I saw a newspaper boy going door-to-door in a horse-drawn wagon. He didn't drop newspapers at any houses that had the word "Jew" scrawled on them.

To anyone who was watching us that morning, we looked like any other Jewish family awake early and going to visit friends or family. We walked quickly down the street to the streetcar, without anyone stopping or questioning us. The only thing that was perhaps a bit unusual was the suitcase that Papa was carrying.

It took us quite a while to get to *Anhalter Bahnof*, the train station near the Central Market in the middle of Berlin. By the time we arrived it was only 6:30 a.m. in the morning, and I was exhausted. I kept thinking about how to say goodbye to my family, and when I would see them again.

All five of us entered the train station. My father went to the ticket office and bought two tickets to Holland and three platform tickets to allow us all on the platform. While waiting patiently for our train to arrive, I watched the trains as they arrived or left from various platforms. None of us spoke. I looked at Mama and saw her fighting back tears. As the train pulled into our platform with smoke billowing out, Mama started sobbing loudly.

Papa helped us into the wooden carriage as soon as the train came to a complete stop. I'm sure he did it quickly so he wouldn't change his mind about sending us away. There was no heat in the third-class compartment and the seats were very hard, cold and uncomfortable. We were all alone. I looked

Golda

Golda with Benno and Heinz

out of the window and saw Mama sobbing, while Papa tried to comfort her. As I looked at her, tears started forming in my own eyes.

"Don't make the children sad," I heard Papa say as he helped Mama into our compartment to see us off. "Be brave like the children." Mama suddenly dried her eyes and looked at us. "Don't let them turn you back, boys. We will follow as soon as we can."

"How strange," I thought. "One minute she wants us to stay and the next minute she wants us to leave."

"Write to us tonight, boys. Write on the train. Write whenever you get a chance," Mama whispered. "Don't leave us without a word from you. We want to hear that you are safe." The next thing I knew, the guard blew the whistle and our parents and Charlie had to get off the train. They gave us each one last hug. We were headed to Holland.

"Goodbye," we cried. And suddenly it was all over. One moment we were a family hugging and kissing each other goodbye, and the next moment we were all alone on the train. We stayed by the window for a long time, waving while the train pulled out of the station. I'll never forget Mama and Papa holding Charlie up so he could wave too, his little face smiling, and his little hand waving goodbye. We watched until they were as small as ants, and we kept waving long after they disappeared. This is the last image I have of my parents and my little brother, and I'll never forget it.

We sat down on the hard, cold seats. I looked at Heinz and I could tell that he was wiping away tears, though he didn't want me to see. He knew that he had to be brave for me.

We still had the compartment all to ourselves. To pass the time, I looked out of the window. At first I saw lots of buildings, but soon we passed through train yards and the city of Berlin. After a while, there were only hedges and fields of snow. I must have dozed for a while; the motion of the train made me sleepy.

"Benno, are you awake?" my brother asked me, nudging my arm. "We're slowing down. I think we must be stopping at a station."

Only a few hours had passed, but it felt like a lifetime. We were two little boys with no family and no home, escaping Germany with only ten marks in our pockets and two train tickets in our hands. Now we were refugees. We were escaping to an unknown world, a world we hoped would be free from Nazi persecution.

"WE'RE STOPPING, THE TRAIN IS STOPPING," my brother said to me quietly. We were sitting far from the centre of the platform as the train pulled in, to make sure the guards standing there did not see us. A train official peered into our compartment and asked to see our tickets. I sat up straight and held my breath. Was he going to tell us to get off the train? He looked at us, he looked at our tickets, then he turned and walked away. The train began moving again. We both breathed a sigh of relief.

Heinz opened the suitcase and took out a pen and post card. "Let's write something

Jewish refugee children from Germany arriving in Holland in 1938

to Mama and Papa. I'll write one half, you write the other," he said.

Waiting to write, I thought about Holland. Heinz and I had often talked about going to Amsterdam, but we never imagined it would be on our own like this. I knew that Amsterdam had a lot of canals and very crowded streets with many very thin, tall buildings. Just a few weeks before, Papa had brought us a book about the city and we had read it eagerly. We didn't know that the train would not stop in Amsterdam, but at the border town of Kleve.

I was uncomfortable, tired and hungry after many hours on the train. I had eaten the sandwiches that Mama had packed. I had looked at a few of the books from our suitcase. I was bored and starting to get scared. I wanted to go home.

Finally, the train stopped at Kleve. Now we didn't know what to do and tried to find someone to help us. Heinz carried our large suitcase and we looked around the busy, crowded train station. We walked outside looking helpless and feeling lost. Night had fallen.

An elderly man in a brown suit approached us. "Are you boys trying to get out of Germany?" he asked. After a few seconds, my brother hesitantly replied, "Yes. We're trying to get to Holland, but we don't know the way."

"You are still in Germany," the man told us. "You have to take a streetcar out to the border." Then he gave us some advice: "If the border guards

Benno and Heinz before they left Germany

in Holland turn you back, the German guards will bring you back to this station. Get back on the train towards Berlin. Get off at the first station, cross the bridge and catch the next train back in the opposite direction. The train across the bridge takes a different route. It will take you to the border guards at Nijmegen, in Holland." This advice was similar to what Papa had told us just that morning.

We thanked the man as the streetcar approached. "Hurry, Benno, there's our streetcar now!" my brother said. We managed to get on with our heavy suitcase and waited for the streetcar to start moving. We held our breaths as the conductor began collecting tickets, but he walked right by us and didn't ask us for a ticket. We were very lucky.

After a little while, the streetcar stopped. The conductor turned to us and asked, "Getting off here?" We got off the streetcar and started walking in the darkness towards the border guards, hoping that this was the right direction.

"You wish to go across the border?" the guard asked Heinz in a loud voice.

"Yes, sir, but we have no passports and we don't know what to do. Can you give us permission to cross the border?"

"Where are your parents?" the second guard asked us. "Do you have friends or family in Holland?"

Before we could answer, the guards turned away from us and started mumbling to each other. Finally, one of the guards, dressed in a brown uniform with a swastika armband, turned to us and said, "We will let you cross the border. Let's see if they'll take you on the other side. If they send you back here, we'll have to put you on a train back to Berlin."

The German guard was a big man, about my father's age, with blond hair and bright blue eyes. He examined our birth certificates, took us to the border, and nodded for us to cross over into Holland. It was completely dark by this time, and we couldn't see very far in front of us. All of a sudden there was a light shining in our faces. Someone screamed, "Halt!" I jumped. I was very scared.

I was shaking as we nervously approached the guards on the Dutch side of the barrier.

"Why were you trying to sneak into Holland?" one of the guards demanded. "You have no papers, no passports."

"We have our birth certificates," Heinz answered.

"Let me see them," one of the guards said gruffly. We pulled them out of our inside coat pockets.

"Only 13, that's very young," one of the guards said out loud. "Look at this one, he's only nine years old! We know why the German guards let you through, because they wanted to get rid of you. But we can't help you get into Holland. You don't have the proper papers. It's very serious to try to enter a country without permission. We will have to send you back where you came from."

I looked at Heinz as the guard pressed a button and a man appeared from the other room. Tears were welling up in my eyes and I kept blinking so they wouldn't start rolling down my cheeks. The guard pointed us to the door. Luckily, Heinz remembered to ask for our birth certificates back. With the certificates safely in our pockets, we started following the border guard back into Germany. I was trying hard not to cry. I was very tired and hungry and didn't want to have to go back across the border.

I remembered what Papa had said just before we left. We should not let them turn us back. We would have to try to get into Holland another way.

JANUARY 29, 1939
KLEVE, GERMANY TO NIJMEGEN, HOLLAND

THE GERMAN GUARDS NODDED to each other when they saw us coming, as if they had expected our return all along. They took us immediately back to the station to be placed on the first train back to Berlin. They warned us that if we tried to cross again at any other border crossing, we would get into serious trouble.

Time dragged as we waited for the Berlin train. The guard waiting with us became very impatient. Finally, the train arrived and we got on. The German guard spoke briefly to the conductor, telling him to watch us and make sure we stayed on the train until we arrived back in Berlin. Luckily for us, there were no armed guards with us on the train. As the train pulled out of the station, I couldn't control myself any more and I started to cry. We were both tired, cold and hungry, and very disappointed that we had not made it out of Germany to safety.

As the train began to slow down, Heinz started to get restless. He got up and began walking along the corridor. "The conductor who has been watching us has gone to another compartment," he said. "We should be able to slip off at this station and try to get on a train to Nijmegen. No one will notice."

Heinz did not wait for the train to come to a complete stop. He grabbed my arm and we jumped from the open doorway, landed on the platform and ran as fast as we could across the bridge. It was hard for me to keep up with him as he had much longer legs than mine.

We had left our large, heavy suitcase on the overhead rack. Now we had nothing to remind us of home, none of the books, favourite toys or photographs that we had packed so carefully. We had no choice. We didn't want the conductor to be suspicious. If he saw us, we figured he would think we had just left to buy some food. Our biggest fear was getting caught.

I watched the train leave, and with it the last remnants of our childhood, until Heinz tugged on my sleeve to keep going. We walked away from the platform to the ticket office and bought two tickets to Nijmegen. "Which platform, please?"

"Number 8. If you hurry you'll catch the train leaving in a few minutes," the clerk told us. Fortunately, the new fare was not expensive because it was only a few stops to Nijmegen. As we got on, the train began to move away from the station. We walked through the passageways, peering into one compartment after another.

"We'll have to hide somewhere," my brother said to me in a panic. "There are Nazi guards out there. It looks like they're searching the train." I looked behind me and could see SS guards marching into each compartment, checking documents. We sped up to keep ahead of them.

"Benno, look!" Heinz said. "This compartment is completely blacked out. I can't get any lights to turn on. If we hide under the seats, maybe they won't find us."

We were in total darkness and immediately slid to the floor and hid under the seats. I couldn't see Heinz; I could just hear his breathing getting heavier. Each time he took in a breath, I thought of us getting caught. We heard footsteps coming closer, getting louder and louder. My heart pounded in my chest. It was beating so fast that I thought it was going to explode. Hot tears fell down my cheeks as the footsteps stopped outside our compartment. Then the guard walked in, the thud of his boots echoing on the floor beside us. Heinz and I held our breath. We thought we were going to burst. After several agonizing seconds, the footsteps started again. They grew quieter as the guard walked away. We let out our breath as quietly as we could. Finally, the train started. We had been lucky again.

I must have dozed off. The next thing I knew, Heinz was shaking me awake. "We can come out now," he said. I crawled out from under my seat and sat down in the darkness. Neither of us had the energy to move or talk. We had been travelling since early morning, and Holland was again within reach.

After a while, the train slowed down. Finally, it came to a complete stop. Heinz peered out of the compartment. He noticed that the station platform was very crowded. Suitcases and other baggage lay everywhere and there were long lines of people, pushing and shoving, trying to get across the border. My brother nudged me to get out of the compartment quickly.

We joined a long line of people and mingled with a large family slowly moving to the front of the line. Neither of us spoke. We kept looking straight in front of us. I was very nervous and looked at Heinz for comfort. Sweat dripped down his forehead. Finally, we reached the border guards. I held my breath, waiting for them to ask us questions, but they didn't say a word. They just nodded to us. Someone else motioned to us to keep moving. Again, no one asked us any questions. I looked at Heinz. He looked at me. We could hardly believe what had just happened. We had just walked into Holland with no one stopping us. It was so easy. The border guards must have thought we were part of another family. It was all over very quickly, and we were free.

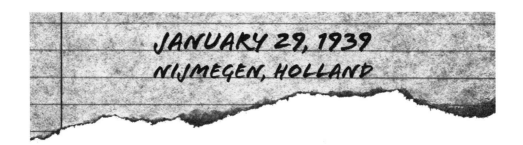

IT WAS ALMOST A MIRACLE! We had made it! We had escaped Nazi persecution. Just a few hundred feet and we were now in a foreign country. We couldn't understand what people were saying; the language sounded very strange, because in Holland everyone speaks Dutch. We had no idea where to go or what to do next.

Heinz and I stood there looking very lost for about 15 minutes. A small man came towards us. He wore round, wire-framed glasses, a coat and a hat. He walked up to my brother and said in broken German, "Are you Jewish refugees from Germany?" How did he know, I wondered, but we were probably very easy to detect. These two tired, hungry, dirty little boys.

"Yes," said Heinz. "Can you help us?"

"I can," the man answered. "Come with me."

Thinking about it today, we had just followed a stranger, not a very good thing to do. However, we really didn't have any choice. We had no one to turn to but each other. We had no one waiting for us in Holland, and nowhere to go. Our parents had told us that this is what would probably happen.

The man opened the door of a taxi. "This seems okay," I thought. I really didn't want to walk anywhere. I was so tired from our journey that I don't think I would have been able to walk for even ten minutes. We were both very dirty from lying on the floor in the train compartment.

The three of us got into the taxi. It pulled away from the station and drove through winding streets for only a few minutes. When the taxi stopped at a house, we got out and followed the man up a steep flight of stairs.

He led us into a room and motioned for us to sit down. After a few minutes of waiting, we were called into another room. When we entered, we saw four men sitting at a long table. They smiled at us, pulled up two extra chairs, and gestured for us to join them. We didn't know what to expect. We were hoping that they would be able to find us somewhere to sleep for the night.

Their German was very good, so we understood their questions. "Why didn't your parents come with you?" they asked.

"We have a little brother and they thought it would be too difficult to travel with him. My parents thought it would be easier if we left first. They plan to follow us as soon as possible," my brother whispered.

"Are you boys hungry? Tired?" We both nodded. We were asked a few more questions about our journey and then we were taken to a house to sleep for the night.

JANUARY 29, 1939
NIJMEGEN, HOLLAND

AS WE WALKED UP THE PATH to a narrow house, a grey-haired woman opened the door. Our guide told her the details of our journey. She smiled and beckoned to us to follow her, and the door closed behind us. We walked along a dimly-lit passageway, its walls filled with paintings. It must have been past midnight, and by this time I was totally exhausted. All I wanted to do was sleep. I didn't care where.

The woman gave us soap and hand towels to wash our hands and faces. She did not speak to us and I wondered if she could speak any German. After a few minutes, she led us into a small dining room that was just off the kitchen. On the table were two egg cups. "Please eat, you must be hungry," she said to us in broken German. I hadn't realized how hungry I was. The last time I had eaten was early in the morning on the first train ride. When we had finished our eggs, she returned from the kitchen and handed us each a glass of steaming hot milk.

I took a sip, expecting it to be too hot, but it was perfect and very delicious. After we had

Young refugees in Holland after their arrival from Germany

finished eating, she told us it was bedtime, which made me happy. We followed her up some narrow stairs to a small, warm room with two single beds. I immediately sat down on one of them. The woman said good night and left, closing the door softly behind her. We were alone in the room with our thoughts. It was the end of a very, very long day, one that seemed to have lasted forever.

As I lay on the soft bed, my mind drifted to Mama and Papa and what they were doing right now in Berlin. "What would Charlie be doing?" I wondered. "Would he realize that we weren't coming back?" The tears rolled down my face as I thought about the life I had left behind.

Heinz sat on my bed and put his arm around me, trying to comfort me. "When do you think we'll see everyone again?" I asked him. "We must think of the future and hope for the best for Mama and Papa and Charlie," he said. I fell asleep very quickly that first night on our own.

Before I knew it, it was morning and time to wake up. "Where am I?" I said. As I looked around the strange bedroom, I didn't recognize it at all. My brother was sitting up already and looking out of the window. "You are in Holland, silly, don't you remember?" he said to me. Slowly, the events of the previous day came back to me.

We made our beds, but mine was really messy, so Heinz helped me. We then quickly got dressed. "Come boys, your breakfast is ready," the woman said as we came downstairs. The meal was very different from what we were used to. Instead of cream of wheat with brown sugar, there were thin slices of bread spread thickly with butter and chocolate sprinkles. It seemed like a real waste of butter to me, especially since butter had been so hard to get in Germany. There were eggs again, very fresh and as delicious as the ones the night before. The cocoa tasted different, too. The food was very rich compared to what we had been eating in Germany. I tried to force myself to eat, but the different food and strange people and places made me lose my appetite. I had a lump in my throat. I missed my family so much.

After breakfast, Heinz asked the woman if we could help with the shopping. "Yes," she said. "Come with me and you can get a look at our pretty town as well. In case you get lost, we live at

21 *Hardstratt*." I don't think she ever told us her name.

We walked out of the two-storey, red brick house, past the neat front garden and hedge, and along the street. The first thing I noticed was the number of soldiers in the street. My brother and I were surprised to see the influence of Hitler's regime in other countries. We thought the trouble was only in Germany. I wondered how safe we were going to be here.

"Do you think there will be a war?" Heinz asked the woman.

"I certainly hope not," she replied.

After we finished helping her with her shopping, she showed us around Nijmegen. The town was beautiful, with lots of windmills everywhere. In the distance we could see a large bridge and a river running straight through the middle of the town.

Back at the house, I turned to Heinz. "What should we do now?" I was used to being at school every day, or at home in the evenings. On the weekends we would all be together, or I would play with one of my friends. I was always busy. Here, there was really nothing to do.

"I'll teach you boys how to play rummy," said the woman's husband whose German was much better than his wife's. This was the first time I realized that someone else was living in the house. He took a pack of playing cards from the side table and the three of us spent a long time learning and then playing cards. This was something we never did at home. I still love to play cards and it all began with this kind man in Nijmegen. To this day, I often relax by playing a game of solitaire at the kitchen table.

Later, we ate lunch. Again, the food was different from what we were used to, and there was a lot of it.

"Let's write a letter to Mama and Papa," I said to my brother after lunch. "We must let them know we're safe." We wrote it and then the two of us walked back into town and mailed our letter. I'm sure Mama and Papa were very happy when they received that letter, knowing that their boys had made it safely out of Germany.

We walked around the neighbourhood again, just because we didn't know what else to do. When we got back, the woman taught us some words in Dutch. This was the first day in my life that I had ever been away from my family, and from Berlin. This Dutch family was very nice to us, but still, I had a big hole in my heart. That emptiness has never left me.

Three days later, we were transferred to a convent in the countryside.

"WHEN YOUR NAME IS CALLED, you will enter the Mother Superior's office to answer her questions," said a loud booming voice. I couldn't see who was speaking. We were lined up at the door of a large house, a convent, surrounded by a fence. Finally, my name was called and I slowly entered the Mother Superior's office.

"Why did you leave Germany?" I looked puzzled, surely she knew why. "Where are your parents?" I didn't know how to explain. Before I got a chance to speak, she started to tell me about the rules at the *Emmakinderhuis* Convent that we had to follow.

"You will be allowed to write to your parents only once each week, on Fridays. These letters will be censored by me, so please do not complain about the treatment here. We will pay the postage. All parcels from your parents will be confiscated. All rules will be followed, especially in making your bed. You will wash before all meals. Bedtime is 7:00 p.m. sharp, lights out at 7:30 p.m. and no talking. You will get up at 7:30 a.m. and wash yourself properly. And then you will make your bed.

The Sister will show you how once, and you will follow her instructions."

I had a bad feeling about this place from the beginning. There were so many rules. The nuns didn't have children of their own, so it seemed to me that they probably didn't know how to handle all of us boys. Suddenly, it felt like a very long time had passed since we had left Berlin and our home. I was already terribly homesick.

"Single file into the dining room," came the order from the Sister in charge of my group. Slowly, one at a time, we all filed in. My brother and I couldn't believe how large the room was. It was painted in a soft cream colour. There were six very long tables. Everything was very clean, even the floor. We stood while we waited for the Mother Superior to enter. I looked around. The convent seemed very cold, too clean and neat to feel like home. No one was allowed to talk while we ate, as speaking at meals was strictly forbidden.

The Mother Superior entered and walked to her seat. We all looked at her and waited for permission to sit down. She finally sat down in her chair and we all followed. The meal was served, some type of meat chopped into very small pieces, with potatoes and cabbage. We were given only forks, no knives. I learned very quickly that we had to eat everything on our plate. We often had beets, which I hated, but we were forced to eat them. To this day, I can't look at a beet without remembering how terrible they tasted!

Jewish refugee children in Holland

The second course was a rice pudding topped with cinnamon. It tasted awful and the texture reminded me of sand. None of us wanted to eat it, but we weren't allowed to leave the table until we had finished all of our food, so I forced down the rice pudding. After the meal, the Mother Superior spoke. "Now boys, all of you over 12 will form a line on the left, while the others will form a line on the right." I walked to the line with my brother. When a Sister told me to go to the other side, I burst into tears. "I promised my Papa that I would not be separated from Benno," said my brother. "He is all that I have and I am all he has."

"It is the rule at *Emmakinderhuis* Convent that the young ones are in one sleeping room and the older boys in another. But under the circumstances, I will allow you to stay with your brother," the Mother Superior said.

There were approximately 60 boys at the convent, no girls, all Jewish refugees from Germany. One of the boys told us that we weren't allowed to have any money. He said, "If you have any money, hide it, otherwise they will take it from you."

"It is the rule at *Emmakinderhuis* that after the midday meal you are to sleep for one hour," the Sister said. No one dared say anything. We walked to the bedroom; it reminded me of a hospital. The bed covers had been folded with a crease down the centre, extending exactly from the middle of the rails at the head of the bed. On every bed was a strange, thin blanket. In Berlin we never used

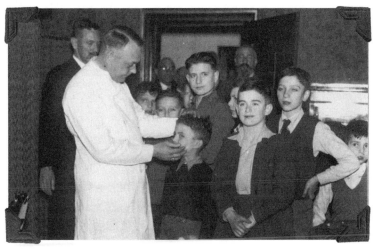

Jewish refugees from Germany receive a medical check-up on their arrival in Holland

blankets, just big feather duvets. A woman came into the room with some of the refugees' luggage. For us, there was a very small case that we had been given in Nijmegen. It held two pairs of pyjamas and a deck of cards from the family that had been so kind to us.

We had never been made to lie down in the middle of the day at home. That one hour seemed like forever. I kept wriggling and couldn't get comfortable.

I didn't think I was going to like life at *Emmakinderhuis*. There were too many rules! I thought my brother and I should run away to some place that would be more fun.

Finally, the hour passed and the nuns showed us how to make our bed. I had never made my bed before; Mama always did it for me. The nuns were very particular about bed-making. If it wasn't done just right, the Sister would come by and rip off all the sheets and blankets and we would have to start all over again.

"The crease must be exactly in the middle, and you can keep making the bed until it is," said the Sister as she pulled my bed apart.

In the afternoon we were taken on a walk, single file, down near the seashore. We were each given a wooden shovel. "Line up on the sand," the Sister ordered, "and listen carefully. Those of you who wish to dig may dig, but remember you must not dig so deep that you reach water. Those who do not wish to dig, follow me."

After a few minutes of digging, I got really bored. How can you make sandcastles without using water? The other choice was to follow the Sister around, which turned out to be just as boring. I still thought that Heinz and I should run away. This place was like a prison.

Everything at *Emmakinderhuis* Convent was precise. The routine was exactly the same every day. After morning bed-making, we went downstairs where a teacher taught us Dutch. In the afternoons after lunch, we had our sleep. We were only allowed to sleep on our left sides. If we accidentally moved to our right, we were woken up and forced to turn over. After our nap, we were given shovels and sent single file down to the beach.

Finally, it was Friday. The morning routine was the same as always. But when we lined up for our wooden shovel, we were given a sheet of notepaper, an envelope and a pencil instead. I had to be careful what I wrote. I let Mama and Papa know how nice it was at *Emmakinderhuis* so they wouldn't worry about me.

FEBRUARY 4, 1939
WIJK AAN ZEE, HOLLAND

WHEN THE WEEKEND ARRIVED, I hoped things would be different, but I didn't get my hopes up. To my surprise, a boy turned to me at breakfast and said "Today we can talk." We also played football, climbed trees and had a lot of fun!

As we walked back to the convent from the football field, I turned to Heinz and said, "When can we make plans to get away from this place?"

"I've been thinking about that," he said, "but I think we have to stay."

I was surprised. I knew he wanted to escape as badly as I did. "I think we should wait for a while," he said. "How would we let Mama and Papa know where we are? And suppose they were on their way to look for us. What would they think if they were told we'd run away? We can't even tell them in a letter. We have to stick it out for a while, Benno. We have to make the week pass somehow, so we can look forward to Saturdays when things are not so bad. Okay?"

"Okay, Heinz," I replied.

The days dragged on. We got through another

week and then enjoyed the weekend, which went by much too quickly. The weeks and weekends contrasted so oddly that it seemed like we were living in two different worlds.

It was a strange place, but nothing bad happened to us until the day my brother bought a ball from one of the boys, even though he wasn't supposed to have any money. The boy who sold him the ball suddenly became ill and one of the Sisters found the money. The boy confessed that Heinz had given it to him to pay for the ball. The Sister and the

Jewish refugee children in transit

Mother Superior began searching Heinz's belongings for any more money. We hadn't spent all the money that Papa had handed to us the morning we'd left Berlin, but they never found it.

After the nuns left, Heinz showed me where he had hidden his money. He had taken out the working movement from the pocket watch that Papa had given us. He had stuffed the money in its place. The money remained hidden in that old watch case long after we left *Emmakinderhuis*.

Near the sixth week of our stay at *Emmakinderhuis*, we heard that we would be leaving soon. I was happy to be leaving, even though I didn't know where we were going. Hopefully, it would be somewhere with fewer rules.

After lunch, the Mother Superior called in a loud voice, "I have been informed that some of you are to be moved." It was true, we were leaving.

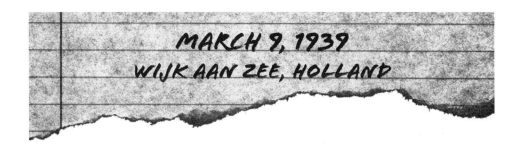

WHEN WE WOKE UP THE NEXT MORNING, someone had packed our belongings for us. I noticed that we had more clothes than we came with. I knew from our parents' letters that they had sent us more than one parcel of clothes, but with the very strict rules we had not seen any of the items. I hoped that the new clothes had come from Mama and Papa.

After breakfast, we collected our things and started to walk with the Jewish Refugee Committee worker to the train station. The walk reminded me of our walk to the station with our parents

Memories of home

Jewish refugee children on a train in 1939

just a few weeks before. Tears welled up in my eyes and I hoped that maybe we would see Mama and Papa at the station with little Charlie. We weren't told where we were being sent. I wondered what the next place would be like.

We entered the train station and in a few minutes we were on a train. The Jewish Refugee Committee worker called us to attention and told us that we were going to an orphanage in Amsterdam. Finally, we were going to Amsterdam, but I didn't like the sound of the word orphanage.

WHEN WE GOT OFF THE TRAIN, we followed the Jewish Refugee Committee worker to a plain-looking building with a wrought iron fence around it. We walked in the front door and I noticed that paint was peeling off the walls and there was thick dust everywhere.

Jewish refugee playing the violin on a train leaving Germany in 1939

"You boys are to go upstairs to your beds," the Matron said as she pointed to the staircase leading up to the dormitories. We reached a dorm. It was awful. Water dripped into the room through a cracked fan. There was dust everywhere. The floors were dirty and the beds untidy.

Some of the boys showed us the bathroom where we washed up. Then we went downstairs to the Matron's office and waited for her to show us around.

I wasn't happy. The windows were filthy, the walls needed to be painted, and the ceilings were grey and dirty. The dining room was also very dirty and the tablecloth had large holes in it. Surprisingly, the food looked alright.

Here we were, starting again, but within minutes of our arrival I wanted to go back to *Emmakinderhuis*. I didn't want to spend any time here in this untidy, dirty, uncared-for place. Even though we had not been happy at *Emmakinderhuis*, it was better than this orphanage, I thought.

After dinner, we undressed and climbed into bed. The water from the ceiling dripped down on my bed. I felt very sorry for myself. I thought our first place was bad, but this one was even worse!

The next morning an alarm bell sounded to wake us up. After breakfast, the Matron told us we would be going to the local Dutch school. Dutch is similar to German, so it was relatively easy for us to learn the language and by the time I left the orphanage, I could speak and understand a bit of Dutch.

The days went by slowly, but at least here we were allowed to write letters as often as we wanted, and no one censored them. I wasn't happy at this place either, but I don't think I would have been happy anywhere but home. Everything was so strange and I felt so alone.

On the third day at the orphanage, we were taken, one at a time, struggling, to the barber's chair. We were strapped in and our heads were shaved to prevent lice from spreading. It was a traumatic experience for me, and for many years afterwards I didn't like to get my hair cut. Whenever I think of this time, I cringe when I recall my head being shaved. After our haircuts, we were given striped uniforms with caps. We looked like convicts. I cried and cried; I thought it was terribly unfair. We were not criminals, were we? Did we deserve to be treated this way? To make matters worse, the other orphans patted our shaved heads and said, "Very nice." I desperately wanted to run away from this place too, but I kept remembering that our parents were trying to escape from Berlin and join us. If we ran away, they would never be able to find us.

One day, a non-Jewish friend of our family from Berlin came to the orphanage. She took Heinz and me to the circus for the afternoon. This was the

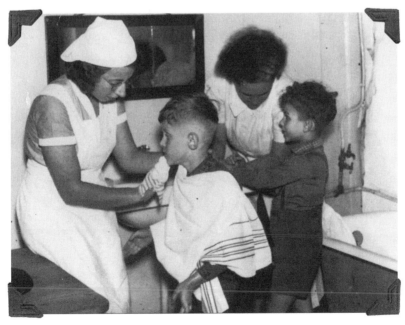

Jewish refugee children after their arrival in Amsterdam in 1939

only connection we'd had with our parents since we'd left. She gave us each some photos from our parents, which we have kept all these years.

I was often very sad and Heinz did his best to cheer me up. I don't know what I would have done without him. Everyone talked about the possibility of war and I was sure it would keep our parents from being able to leave Berlin. I had a feeling that it would be a very long time, if ever, before we would all be reunited.

A few weeks later, while I was cleaning my boots, Heinz ran up to me and said, "Benno, I just heard the Matron say that we're leaving again. Papa and Mama are not coming, but they've arranged for us to get away from here!"

"That's great," I said. "When do we get out?" I didn't think to ask where we were going.

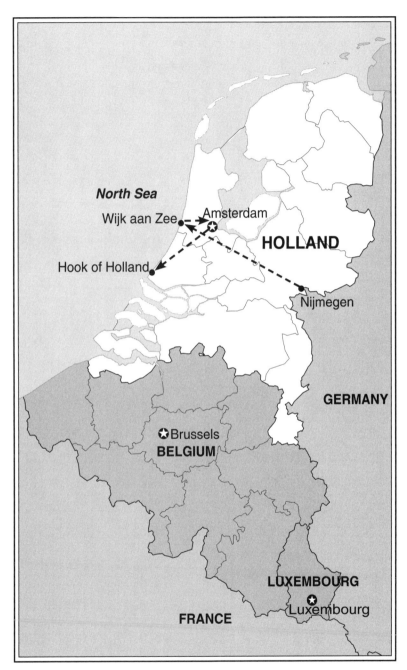

Benno and Heinz's journey to the Hook of Holland

NOVEMBER 1938 TO AUGUST 1939
ENGLAND

PEOPLE IN EUROPE AND THE UNITED STATES were shocked at newspaper reports of burning synagogues and broken glass, but the United States and Canada still refused to take in refugees.

In England, the Jewish Refugee Committee persuaded the Government to let in up to 10,000 unaccompanied children under the age of 18 from Germany, Austria and Czechoslovakia. Private citizens and organizations guaranteed to pay for each child's care and education. The Government let the children enter on travel visas, with the understanding that they would leave after the war.

The first children's transport, or *Kindertransport,* arrived in Harwich, England in December 1938. The last transport from Germany left in late August 1939, just before the war started. Most of the children left by train from major cities in central Europe to ports in Belgium and Holland. From there, the children travelled across the English Channel, mainly to Harwich. The children of the *Kindertransport* were sent to many parts of England, Scotland, Wales and Northern Ireland. This rescue operation saved a total of 9,600 children. None were accompanied by parents; a few were babies carried by older children.

APRIL 18, 1939
THE HOOK OF HOLLAND, HOLLAND

AT BREAKFAST THE MATRON CALLED eight names, including my brother's and mine. As we walked to the train station, I found my old calendar in my jacket pocket and counted the days that we had been in Amsterdam. It had been six weeks, the same amount of time that we had been at *Emmakinderhuis*. We had just settled in and now we were on the move again.

After the war, I learned that the orphanage we lived in had been destroyed by the Germans. We eight boys were the only survivors. If we had remained in Holland, we would have been sent to a concentration camp and probably not have survived.

We boarded the train at Amsterdam. Again, we had no idea where we were being sent. I was in one compartment with Heinz and our friend, Eli. The other five boys were together in the next compartment. Heinz and Eli started to talk about where we were being sent. We were all very scared, and we talked in detail about running away. I pulled out an old map from my pocket and we thought that we could get to Turkey or Iraq, and then to Palestine and safety.

Jewish children escaping Nazi Germany by train, 1939

We were frightened of getting caught, and had little money between us. We had heard about some boys who had tried to run away and had been caught by the police. We therefore decided it was too dangerous and we would have to go wherever we were sent.

After about four hours, the train stopped and we were all told to get off. I was scared; no one had told us anything. We had arrived in the port town known as the Hook of Holland. There were lots of children, all refugees, and none of us knew what would happen to us. I was very worried. I kept as close to my brother as possible. We asked everyone around us if they knew where we were going. England, was the answer. How did our parents arrange this? We never found out. As we walked towards the crowd, we saw a big ferry in port, full of children. Finally, we were told to get on board. Hesitantly, I followed the children in front of me.

We walked onto a gangplank to the deck of the ferry where we sat together with other boys and girls. The ferry finally moved out of the harbour and gathered speed. Heinz and I walked to the rail to watch the departure from the dock. As Holland faded away, we looked at each other. We had no idea what to expect of the next leg of our journey. We didn't know whether we would ever return, or if we would see our parents again. Each move we made took us further away from our family.

Jewish refugees from Germany boarding a boat for England in 1939

It was already April, but the waves in the English Channel were very, very rough. Many of the children were seasick, but luckily we were not. I don't remember much else about the boat ride, except that we were fed soup and bread. The bread was soft, white English bread that looked like cake. We played games to pass the time and, soon enough, we saw the White Cliffs of Dover in the distance. We landed in Harwich that evening, but it took a while before we were let off the ferry. Thinking about it now, I realize that we eight boys probably weren't on the passenger list and the authorities had to straighten out the confusion. The number of children on the list had to match the number on the ferry. It took a couple of hours for negotiations to be completed.

Benno and Heinz in England in 1939

While we waited to be allowed off the ferry, we peered over the rail at this strange country. I wondered about life in England. What were the people like? Would I be able to talk with them? What would school be like? There were lots of people waiting at the shore, meeting someone they had promised to take care of. I wondered who would take care of us.

APRIL 18, 1939
FELIXSTOWE, ENGLAND

AT LAST WE WERE ALLOWED OFF THE FERRY. We stood on the dock at Harwich, England, and waited for someone to come and get us. I looked around at our strange new surroundings and listened to another strange new language. I wondered if here we could have a new life, free of persecution.

We were taken to a large hall where we waited until our names were called, and then we took a short bus ride to Felixstowe. We were to stay in a hostel. Our hostel warden was a refugee from Vienna, and he spoke German.

Jewish children escaping to England in 1939

Young Jewish refugees from Germany shortly after their arrival in England

The streets of this new town were nothing like Berlin, or even Nijmegen or Amsterdam. The houses seemed smaller, the cars were driven on the wrong side of the street, and the shops were crowded together.

Upon arriving at the hostel, we were immediately shown to our dormitory where we unpacked and put our few clothes into the cupboard. We would eat all our meals at a house across the street which belonged to the hostel. The hostel warden and his wife were responsible for us, and made our life very pleasant. It was a nice change after the strict rules and lack of care we had lived with for nearly three months.

There weren't enough private homes to accommodate all the children who arrived in England from Nazi-occupied Europe on what had become known as the *Kindertransport*. Many children, like us, lived in hostels, while others lived in group homes, or with foster families, or on farms. The Jewish Refugee Committee hoped that we would only have to stay in the hostel for a few months, and that our parents would be able to come and get us. We all shared that hope.

Heinz and Benno in 1939

The Committee had trouble finding the money to support us all. War came in September of 1939 and there were many children who were unlikely to see their parents until after it was all over. As it turned out, the Committee looked after me for five years. I owe a great deal to the Committee and the hostels. As a child, I took their help for granted, but looking back I can see that they did everything they could to help us all through a very difficult and lonely time.

For the first three weeks after our arrival, we were allowed to play and just have fun. Getting settled in England was very different from our life in Holland.

Letter writing was not controlled or censored, and we finally heard from our parents. It was a huge relief, and a great source of joy when we got their letter. They were pleased that we were now safe in England and had been able to find a place where we were happy. In those few months before the war began, we got letters from them all the time and they sent us lots of photographs of family from our home in Berlin. We couldn't wait for mail time every day. I wrote to them all the time, too. I remember writing to Mama and telling her about the English breakfast cereal. I thought cornflakes were a very strange thing for breakfast, but I liked them! I read and re-read every letter my parents sent me. Those letters were the only connection I had to my family.

In Germany, school was only in the mornings, but in England we had to go to school all day. Our English began to improve. We started making friends with English children and visited them at their homes. Days passed in England, happy days that made all the bad days seem to fade away. Our hair grew in again and we felt much more like ourselves.

MAY 29, 1939
CLAYDON, ENGLAND

ONE DAY, THE HOSTEL WARDEN WALKED into the large room where we gathered after school. He looked very sad. "Boys, I have some news for you. I have to send some of you to a place called Barham House. It's in Claydon, on the east coast of England. We need to make room for some other refugees."

The following morning, May 29, 1939, most of us packed our things. The six-week time period had come again. Just as we were getting comfortable with the rules, we were forced to leave. I couldn't believe we would have to start over once again. We boarded the bus with heavy hearts.

We drove in the sunshine through beautiful countryside until we reached Claydon. We would live in houses according to our age. Each house had a name and I was sent to Baldwin House, while Heinz was sent to Brentnall House. For the first time since leaving home, Heinz and I would live apart. For some reason, I accepted the change. I discovered that some boys from *Emmakinderhuis* Convent and two boys I had met on the ferry were in my house.

My very first question upon arriving was about the rules. Each new move meant new rules and expectations, and just when I got used to them, we moved again. The boys told me that school was only in the mornings, Monday to Friday, and there was a system where you could earn points for things like tidiness and good behaviour. "Maybe I'll be able to stay here for a while," I thought.

We got used to life at the hostel very quickly. Except for the fact that we didn't have our parents with us, we started to feel like regular kids again.

Most of the boys came from either Austria or Germany. One of them showed me around and I discovered that the hostel was pretty self-contained. There was a bakery, laundry, boot repair shop and tailor. The only thing that was missing was a barber shop. That explained why all the boys had such long hair!

There were no strict rules about going to school. Attendance was never taken, and I think because of that, everyone went every day. The only unusual class for me was the one where we learned English. Otherwise, school seemed just like school back in Germany.

Our afternoons were free. We built things, played games, and spent time with our friends. The days passed quickly; soon we were well into the summer and nearing my tenth birthday. I wrote home often. Heinz and I were both enjoying ourselves and the very difficult days faded a bit from our memories.

German refugee children at school in England in 1939

Earning money became important to us. Clothes and toys were given to us, and we also got a very small allowance, but we had nothing of our own. We traded anything we had to earn money for things like going to the movies. The hostel had leaders, called prefects, chosen from among the children. I became a prefect and earned two pence (worth approximately 10 cents today) a week for doing work around the hostel and supervising the other boys. My job was to make sure that the boys made their beds and their belongings were tidy. If they didn't follow the rules, they could lose their allowance or part of it.

One day, my friends and I found blackberry bushes and I thought up a great plan to make some extra money. We made fruit juice and sold it for half a penny a cup to the boys who played soccer.

We also got into lots of mischief, including making cigarettes out of dried leaves wrapped in toilet paper. I was ten years old when I started smoking, not realizing what an unhealthy habit it is.

My favourite possession was a bicycle that I had found dumped in a ditch. It only had one pedal, which made it very difficult to ride, but I did it anyway. I learned to ride that bike and swim at Barham House. There was a small river running through the grounds and we swam whenever the weather was hot. We built a raft, and had many great adventures. I remember trying to parachute off the fire escape of one of the buildings from three floors up, holding onto a blanket tied to my belt. Luckily, I didn't get hurt, and I didn't get caught!

Sometimes we were quarantined, as there was often an epidemic of diphtheria or chicken pox going through the hostel. During those times, we couldn't go into the local village.

One afternoon, two famous table tennis players, Victor Barna and Richard Bergman, came to the hostel. They had been invited to demonstrate their skill in playing table tennis. That evening, Heinz and I wrote to our parents to tell them about the demonstration. We wrote a letter together in order to save one envelope, as there was a big market for stamped envelopes and we could trade them for other things we wanted.

It wasn't long before my clothes started to get too small for me to wear. I traded some of our saved–

up envelopes for some larger clothes. We also got clothes from the Jewish Refugee Committee, donated by the big department store, Marks and Spencer. We were very lucky to be cared for during those years when we were alone and too young to work.

Jewish refugees from Germany in a hostel in England

Time seemed to be passing very quickly now. It was almost August, nearly my birthday, and we were having fun. Sometimes I was sad and homesick, but I was getting used to being alone.

One day, Heinz and I received a long, unexpected letter from our grandfather in the United States. We looked at the unusual stamp for a while before we dared open the letter.

When we had left Berlin, our parents had suggested that we try to make our way to our grandfather, but this was the first time we had heard from him. He wrote that it would be very difficult for him to meet the requirements for our immigration to the United States. However, he did include $5.00 (worth approximately $50.00 today) for each of us. The money was going to make my birthday a big success.

When we heard that we were not going to go to the United States, we soon got over not being able to leave the hostel. One thing I learned quickly as a refugee was to accept disappointment as part of life.

My birthday, August 6, fell on the weekend. That Saturday morning was bright and sunny. I got up early to get ready for our big adventure. I had promised my friends that I would take them all into Ipswich, the city closest to Barham House, to see a movie. This was a big treat for all of us. Later that night, lying in bed, I realized that I had spent all of my 'wealth' during just one day. What a great day it was; I had no regrets.

A few days later, a sign appeared outside the hostel office door: "Blackout Test to be Held".

These tests were held in case of war. In preparation, we were each given some black cloth to cover the windows. This would block out any light and make us invisible to German airplanes. It looked like war was coming soon.

1939
THE OUTBREAK OF WAR IN EUROPE

HITLER BEGAN HIS CAMPAIGN to take over Europe by seizing control of Austria in March of 1938. Next, he demanded that Czechoslovakia surrender its ethnically German regions. Major European powers Britain and France agreed to his demands, hoping war could be avoided. Hitler promised that he had "no further territorial claims in Europe", and British Prime Minister Neville Chamberlain claimed he had achieved "peace for our time". Six months later, Hitler broke the pact and annexed the rest of Czechoslovakia.

On September 1, 1939, Germany invaded Poland in a massive surprise attack, marking the beginning of World War II. In 1940, Hilter's army invaded Denmark, Norway, Holland, Luxembourg, Belgium and France. After the Nazis occupied these countries, they imposed their racist policies and brutal practices across the continent.

War spread across the globe, with fighting centered primarily in Europe and Asia. The Allies, including Canada, the United States, Britain and the Soviet Union, fought together to stem the territorial ambitions of the main Axis powers—Nazi Germany, Fascist Italy and Imperial Japan. It was not until May of 1945 that the Allies were able to liberate Europe from Nazi oppression.

ON SEPTEMBER 3, WE WERE GIVEN some bad news. England, which had kept us so safe, was now at war with Germany.

The first change for us was that letters across international borders now had to go through the Red Cross, and would be censored. Suddenly, home seemed much further away. We heard air raid sirens and wondered if we were going to be bombed.

War cast its shadow, but the days passed almost as usual at Barham House. We had pillow fights, room fights and house fights. The football team played the villagers one weekend and won the match. The next weekend, our team played Ipswich and lost.

We stayed healthy, happy and busy, swimming, boating, cycling and playing table tennis. We often wrote to our parents through the Red Cross, and we heard from them every two weeks or so.

Late in September, we got an order to dig trenches, to hide us from enemy troops in the event of an invasion. At first it was a lot of fun, but after a while our muscles began to hurt. We finished the first trench after a few days.

I thought our hard work would end when the trenches were finished. Then, a notice was posted on the hostel door about catching rats and mice, which were eating our food. We were to catch and kill as many as we could. One penny would be paid for a mouse's tail and two pennies for a rat's tail.

Everyone was given traps. I placed mine, but for some strange reason the bait was always stolen and the animal got away, or else the baited trap stayed untouched. I wasn't very good at this job. Either someone was sabotaging my traps, or the rats and mice were too clever to get caught!

NOVEMBER 1939 TO MAY 1940
CLAYDON, ENGLAND

HEINZ'S FOURTEENTH BIRTHDAY was on November 24, and he celebrated much the same way as I had. But at fourteen, there would be no more school for him; he had to earn a living. The Nazis had prevented him from getting an education, and he hadn't gone to school in England long enough to qualify for any job other than farming. He wasn't happy about working on a farm. Not long after his birthday, he

Heinz and Benno in 1940

told me he was leaving for Birmingham to take a job as a tailor's apprentice. He was going to learn to become a tailor like our father. Heinz lived in a refugee hostel in Birmingham for three years and met his future wife there.

After all we had been through together, we were now being separated. It was hard on me. I went to the train station with him and felt very sad saying goodbye. I didn't know that it would be many, many months before I would see my brother again. We wrote to each other often, as he settled down in his new life in Birmingham. He said that the work was interesting and, from his letters, he seemed happy.

Around this time we found out that all Germans living in England were considered enemy aliens. Enemy

Heinz (bottom right) in Birmingham, England

aliens were not allowed to live by the sea in case they saw war manoeuvres and passed this information to the Germans. I am sure that is why we once again heard rumours that we were to be moved. I don't know who started the rumours, but they worried me. "We're going to a place called Wallingford," we were told.

Wallingford was a prison for young offenders near Oxford, further inland. About 30 of us were told to pack our bags and we were moved there. We stayed for another six weeks, separated from the inmates and juvenile delinquents. We had been sent there temporarily because the hostel in Leeds where we were headed was not quite ready for us.

By this time, I had lived in three different places in Holland and three places in England. I was about to move to Leeds, to another hostel where I stayed for three-and-a-half years.

English children started ariving from the cities as their parents sent them away from the bombed-out cities on the coast. We weren't bombed ourselves, but still we felt the war closing in on us. My English was getting quite good, and the English children were used to me and to the other refugees, but our accents and our names marked us as different. Even today, I still speak with an accent.

The war continued. It seemed to go on forever. Most of us had not heard from our parents, so news was the most important event in our lives. The last letter we ever received was in 1941.

1940 TO 1945
LEEDS, BIRMINGHAM AND LONDON, ENGLAND

MY MEMORIES OF THE NEXT FEW YEARS flow into each other. The longer the war lasted, the more anxious I became to learn about the fate of my family. My parents were supposed to have come and taken us away with them many years before. As the years went by, I began to doubt that I would ever see them and my little brother Charlie again.

The hostel in Leeds was located on Stainbeck Lane and, again, it was very different from anything else I had experienced up to this point. It was an Orthodox Jewish institution, and it had its own synagogue. There were about 150 boys between the ages of nine and 15 years old. We lived in dormitories, 10 boys to a room. We went to synagogue three times a day to pray, and we learned a lot about being Jewish. I had to cover my head with a *kipah*, at all times. Even though my family was not religious, I had no choice but to observe the rules.

In August 1942, I turned 13 years old. I was happy that Heinz joined me as I celebrated my *bar mitzvah* in the hostel with two other boys whose birthdays were a few days apart from mine. I hadn't seen Heinz for over two years. He arrived and attended synagogue with me on the Saturday morning, *Shabbat*, when no work is done. After synagogue, we pulled chairs up to the apple trees in the orchard and ate the apples right off the tree, even though we weren't allowed to pick the apples on *Shabbat*!

In England, boys wore short pants and got their first long trousers when they were 13. I didn't have any, and it was my dream to get a pair. One day, I found a pair of dirty, old long pants thrown out in the garbage. I washed them and tried to iron them by putting them under my mattress. They were damp and wrinkled, but I wore them proudly.

In June 1943, I left Leeds and school. I was almost 14. Like Heinz, my schooling had been interrupted

Benno's Bar Mitzvah, August 1942

and it was time for me to get a job and support myself. I never formally returned to school.

I wanted to leave Leeds and the hostel, and be closer to my brother. Heinz left his hostel in Birmingham to make room for me there, and lived elsewhere in Birmingham for a while. Later, he moved to London, where he got married in 1945. I came to London for the wedding, which took place at City Hall. We planned to go to the theatre as a celebration afterwards, but Heinz forgot the tickets and he had to take a taxi back home to get them. We made it to the play just in time. What a special day that was!

Heinz married Fella in 1945

By the time I was 14 years old, I had a job doing war work in an engineering factory and lived all by myself in Birmingham. I was earning enough money to support myself. When I finally moved to London to be close to my brother again, I managed to find a room opposite the one where he and Fella were living. Though we had both changed, he was my only family.

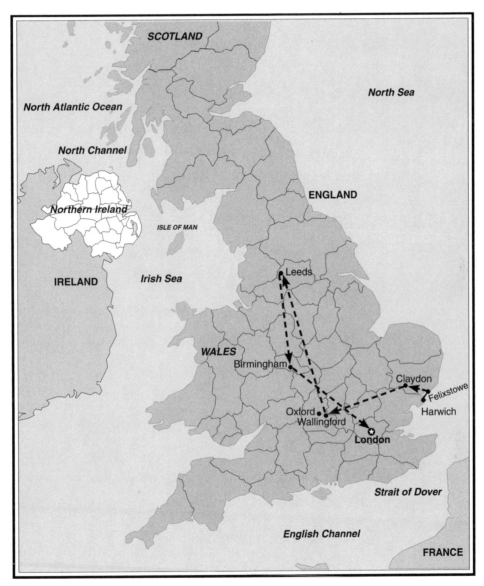

Places Benno lived in England, 1939–1945

1945
EUROPE: THE AFTERMATH

WHEN THE WAR ENDED IN 1945, the world discovered the full extent of Hitler's hatred of the Jews. Of the 9,000,000 Jews in Europe before the war, 6,000,000 men, women and children had been murdered by the Nazis. Although reports of the extermination of Jews had reached the outside world, no action was taken to help the Jews of Europe until the concentration camps were liberated at the very end of the war. The *Kindertransport* was one of the few exceptions.

Nazi Germany's war against the Jews is called the Holocaust, one of the darkest chapters in the history of mankind.

After the war, the British Government's original immigration restrictions were eased and children of the *Kindertransport* who had lost their parents were allowed to remain as British citizens. Some children emigrated to Israel, the United States, Canada and Australia. Most would never again see their families, who were murdered during the Holocaust.

Of the children who were trapped in Nazi-occupied Europe after 1939, over 1,500,000 were murdered by the Nazis. The *Kindertransport* saved approximately 9,600 children from almost certain death.

1945
LONDON, ENGLAND

IN APRIL 1945, WE HEARD THE NEWS of the liberation of the concentration camps. Then we heard that the war in Europe finally ended on May 8, 1945. All of us celebrated wildly. At long last the destruction, fighting and killing were over, but I was still scared. What would I find out? How would I find my parents and little brother? What would happen if I didn't find them? What would my brother and I do? I had been hoping for so long that one day we would be a family again.

Heinz and I searched for our family. We asked everyone we met who had been freed from concentration camps if they knew our parents. We heard nothing. We asked through the Red Cross. There was no official statement or death certificate. We had to move forward and continue our lives without really knowing where our parents and Charlie were.

One day, my brother met a man we knew from Berlin. He had been one of our neighbours and he told Heinz that our family had been taken to Auschwitz, a concentration camp, in March 1943. He was on the same transport. He said that they had been gassed immediately upon arrival.

Jews arriving at Auschwitz in May 1944

My father would have been 45 years old, my mother 37 years old and Charlie just a boy of seven. They were selected for death because the Nazis decided that they were incapable of hard labour in Auschwitz. We were not certain whether this information was correct, and always hoped that at least Charlie had survived.

After the war ended, we learnt that over 1,500,000 Jewish children were murdered by the Nazis and we gave up hope that Charlie had survived. We knew then that we were truly orphans and would have to make our own way. It was very traumatic for us to realize that we were all alone. Heinz was already married, but I was truly on my own. Most of the boys I had spent the last few years with were in the same position. There were only a few who were lucky enough to be reunited with their families.

I did not live through the worst horrors of the Holocaust. I was not put into a concentration camp. I did, however, go through more pain and suffering, loneliness and sadness than anyone should have to face in a lifetime. Even today, when I talk about those times, I cannot think about my parents or little brother and what happened to them, without getting upset.

On my 16th birthday, August 6, 1945, the atom bomb was dropped on Hiroshima. Soon after, fighting ended in the Pacific. With the war over, I realized that my life had been saved. Was I grateful for this? It is difficult for me to be sure. I felt guilty that Heinz and I had survived and that our family had not. In my rational moments I knew that I was indeed fortunate, and I realized why our parents had sent us away to safety.

England may not have been too eager to accept refugees in 1939, but in 1947 the British Government again showed kindness. Parliament passed an act that gave immediate citizenship to children who had come to England with the *Kindertransport*, and had lost their parents. After the turbulence of the war, I tried to adapt to my new life. To blend into English society we, like many others, changed our German-sounding name to an English one.

My family had not been in a position to make plans for their future or mine. We would not have chosen to leave Germany except for the circumstances of Nazi persecution, which changed our lives. My brother and I were among the most fortunate, whose lives were saved.

1949–1955
LONDON, ENGLAND

AFTER THE WAR, I MET a young English girl who had been sent by her family to the countryside to escape the German bombing. We met at a Jewish discussion club in London in 1949. Her name is Rita and we have been happily married for 54 years. We have three children and seven grandchildren.

Benno married Rita in 1953

Our daughter was born in 1955, two years later. I was a young man of 26 when I brought Rita and my newborn daughter home from the hospital. As I looked at my baby, so innocent, I felt my life change. I was the father now, with my own family, and although I knew I must look forward for my daughter's sake and not back, I felt closer to my own father than I had in a long time. Even so, it wasn't until she turned nine years old, and I saw how young she still was, that I realized how truly difficult it must have been for my parents to send us away to safety. At long last, I understood the sacrifice they had made.

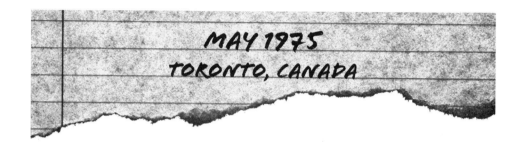

I BELIEVE I AM SAFE IN CANADA, but the seeds of hatred exist even here. My car is parked at the front of my house in the driveway. As I open the front door to go to work, I see that my car has been spray painted. As I look closer I see a large black swastika has been painted on the side of the car.

I call Rita to come outside. Neither of us can believe what we see. After all these years, after all I've endured, the life I have built for my family, there is a swastika on my car, a symbol of Nazi hate.

I immediately drive my car to a body shop. I don't want anyone else, children, friends or neighbours, to see what some criminals have done. How could they have done this to me? After all I have gone through?

A few days later, I pick up my car. It looks different now. It's dark brown, and I tell myself it needed a paint job, but really I'd just wanted to cover up the graffiti as fast as I could.

I didn't need to be reminded of everything I'd gone through. Such things you never forget.

AS I WALK IN THE FRONT DOOR, I notice a letter with a Swiss stamp addressed to me, lying on the hall table. I wonder who it could possibly be from. I turn the letter over and see it is from the Red Cross. Is it possible I have finally received some information about my family?

I had written to the Red Cross many years before, but now finally they had obtained lists from the German Archives of victims in Auschwitz. My parents and little brother, Charlie, were amongst them.

The Nazis had been very diligent in keeping precise records of their victims, but it had taken many, many years for the German authorities to release this information. There were no death certificates, but the letter did state that Papa, Mama and Charlie had been gassed upon arrival in Auschwitz.

Heinz and I had lived for many years with the belief that they had been killed, but seeing the information in print for the first time confirmed our worst fears.

NOVEMBER 23, 2001
TORONTO, CANADA

MY GRANDDAUGHTER TURNS NINE TODAY. We all sit around the dining room table for Friday night dinner. I know that tonight is the night I must tell my story. I take a deep breath as I pause to gather my thoughts. I was a boy of nine when my parents sent me away. How can a child of nine understand why parents would ever send their own children away?

My wife, Rita, starts to light the *Shabbat* candles. As we begin to eat the *challah* and chicken soup, I turn to my granddaughter and say, "I have something to talk to you about tonight. This is not easy for me to discuss, but in January 1939 I was sitting at the dinner table with my parents and brothers exactly like we are tonight. My parents told us that my brother and I were to leave our home in Berlin on our own within the next few days. Can you imagine if this were the last Friday night we were to be together as a family?"

EPILOGUE

I HAVE TOLD MY STORY IN AN EFFORT to fight ignorance, prejudice and intolerance. We must be sure that the world does not repeat the events that led to World War II.

Through this book I have tried to honour my family and the memory of the 6,000,000 who died at the hands of the Nazis. I hope that their deaths have not been in vain. By remembering the experiences of the Holocaust, we try to ensure it is never forgotten.

My childhood was not unusual for that time in history. What was unusual was that I survived. Over 1,500,000 Jewish children like me died, and are not able to tell their story. In a desperate act of love, my parents placed my brother and me on a train out of Germany. Through the support and kindness of strangers, the two of us were saved together with other children on the *Kindertransport*.

As a child I found it very hard to accept what my parents had done for me. I wanted desperately to be with my family, wherever they were, not in a strange country with strange people, all alone.

As I grew to adulthood, I realized how lucky I was, but I often wondered, why me? Why was I saved when so many others were not? As with other survivors, the pain and sorrow of my childhood still lives with me.

What I went through has made me who I am today, and it has influenced my daughters as well. That is why, when each of my children and grandchildren turn nine years old, I feel it is important to tell them my story. I am thankful that I have been able to do so, through the support, encouragement and love of my family.

My parents gave us life twice, once when we were born and again when they sent us away to safety.

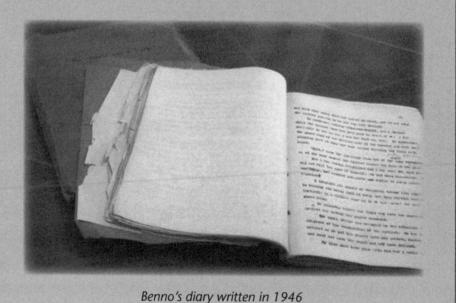

Benno's diary written in 1946

APPENDIX

GLOSSARY

Anti-Semitism: Hatred or persecution of the Jewish people.

Auschwitz: A Nazi concentration camp (the largest) located in Poland, near Krakow. Established in 1940, it became a centre of mass murder during the Nazi Holocaust.

Bar Mitzvah/Bat Mitzvah: The 'coming of age' when a Jewish boy turns thirteen or a Jewish girl turns twelve and takes his/her rightful place in the congregation.

Blitzkrieg: Lightning war. Quick, surprise strikes by mobile forces in light tanks, with airborne and infantry support.

Challah: A loaf of yeast-leavened bread, usually braided, traditionally eaten by Jews on the Sabbath, holidays and other ceremonial occasions.

Concentration camp: These prison camps were an essential part of the Nazi reign of terror. The single largest group of prisoners in these camps was Jews. Disease, starvation, crowded and unsanitary conditions, abuse, brutality and the random murder of prisoners, including those considered unfit for work, were a daily part of life in these camps.

Dachau: Established in 1933, it was the first of the Nazi concentration camps.

Death camp: Nazi extermination centres where Jews and other victims were systematically killed as part of Hitler's Final Solution.

Final Solution: The Nazi plan to eliminate all the Jews of Europe.

Führer: Leader. Adolf Hitler's title in Nazi Germany.

Hitler, Adolf (1889–1945): Nazi party leader, German Chancellor, 1933–1945. Rose to become the supreme leader of Germany.

Hitler Youth: A Nazi youth group established in 1922. Membership was compulsory after 1939.

Holocaust: The systematic planned extermination of approximately 6,000,000 European Jews by the Nazis during World War II.

Israel: The modern-day Jewish State, established in the Jewish people's ancestral homeland in 1948, following the Holocaust.

Jewish Refugee Committee: Set up to assist in the rescue of thousands of Jews from persecution, war and statelessness.

Kinder: Children who traveled to safety on the Kindertransport.

Kindertransport: Children's transport. The movement to evacuate children to England following Kristallnacht. The first children arrived on December 2, 1938. Through the Kindertransport, 9,600 children were brought to safety.

Kipah: (also yarmulke or skullcap) A traditional head covering worn by Jews.

Kristallnacht: Night of the Broken Glass. On this night, November 9–10, 1938, over 250 synagogues and 7,500 Jewish shops were destroyed, more than 100 Jews were killed, and tens of thousands of Jews were sent to concentration camps.

Nazi: A member of the National Socialist Party, which ruled Germany from 1933–1945 under Adolf Hitler.

Nuremberg Laws: Laws announced by Hitler at the Nuremberg Party Conference, defining "Jew" and regulating discrimination and persecution. The "Reich Citizenship Law" deprived all Jews of their civil rights, while the "Law for the Protection of German Blood and German Honour" made close personal relationships between Jews and Germans punishable by imprisonment.

Refugee: A person who seeks shelter in another country from war, disaster or persecution.

Torah: A sacred scroll containing the Five Books of Moses.

Shabbat: (also Shabbos) Seventh day of the Jewish week—from sundown Friday to nightfall Saturday—during which Jews are commanded to rest from work activities.

SS: Storm Troopers. These military units of the Nazi Party, also known as Brownshirts, enabled Hitler's rise to power.

Synagogue: Jewish house of worship.

Swastika: An ancient religious symbol that became the official symbol of the Nazi Party. Now banned in Germany, the swastika is still used by neo-Nazis around the world as a symbol of hate.

Third Reich: The Nazi regime from 1933–45.

1929
» Benno is born in
Berlin, Germany.

1938
» Family shop and home are
destroyed during *Kristallnacht*.

1939
» Benno and Heinz cross the
border into Holland.
» The boys escape to England
on the *Kindertransport*.

Family
Timeline

1929   1939

Historical
Timeline

1938
» *Kristallnacht:* Nazi-organized,
nationwide anti-Jewish riots.
» The *Kindertransports* begin.

1933
» Nazi Party takes
power in Germany.
» Adolf Hitler is
appointed Chancellor
of Germany.

1935
» Anti-Jewish Nuremberg
Laws are enacted.

1939
» Start of World War II.
» Nazis begin to round up
Jews for mass deportation,
slave labour and eventual
slaughter.

1942
» Benno has his *Bar Mitzvah*.

1943
» Max, Golda and Charlie are sent to Auschwitz concentration camp.

1945
» Benno and Heinz learn that their family has been murdered in Auschwitz concentration camp.
» Benno writes his original manuscript.

1940 — **1948**

1945
» Survivors from concentration camps are liberated.
» End of World War II.

1942
» Nazi leaders meet in Berlin to discuss the "Final Solution" to the Jewish Question.

1947
» The United Nations endorses the establishment of a homeland for the Jewish People.

1948
» The modern-day State of Israel is created.

QUESTIONS FOR DISCUSSION

Sadly, racial, ethnic, and cultural hatred and intolerance are not just history; they are current events.—Steven Spielberg, film director

1. Between 1933 and 1938, the Nazi government passed the Nuremberg Laws banning Jews like Benno from schools, parks, swimming pools, movie theatres, skating rinks and other public places. Their German citizenship was taken away, and they found themselves persecuted and isolated from the wider community.

Why do you think countries around the world stood by and let this happen? What did countries like Canada do to oppose these acts of prejudice and discrimination by the German government?

2. Through the passing of the Nuremberg Laws, many children, including Benno and Heinz, had the bitter experience of being excluded and segregated.

Discuss what it means to be an outcast, someone who is not accepted by his/her peers. In what other periods in history have people been excluded because of who they were, rather than what they had done?

What would you do if you saw your friends making someone feel unwelcome at your school, or treating them differently?

3. After *Kristallnacht,* **the British Government allowed the** *Kindertransport* **to bring 9,600 unaccompanied Jewish children from Europe to safety. Consider how difficult it must have been for parents to send their children off by themselves to safety, not knowing whether they would ever see them again.**

What advice might your parents give to you if you were going away and they were fearful for your safety?

4. The German government allowed the children travelling on the *Kindertransport* **to bring only one suitcase and one backpack containing items for personal use. No jewellery, cameras or valuables were allowed, and no money in excess of 10 Marks.**

What would you pack that would comfort you and remind you of home? What objects hold particular importance to you and why?

5. Once in England, Benno and the other *Kindertransport* **children had to adapt to new customs, learn a new language and build a new life.**

What challenges do you think you would have to face adapting to a new country, such as living in a hostel or foster home, eating strange food, speaking a new language and living in an unfamiliar environment?

Have you ever had to move to a new country? Do you have experiences to share?

6. VE Day on May 8, 1945 marked the end of the war in Europe, and was a time of great joy. However, for many refugees the end of the war brought the realization that they would never see their families again. Benno and Heinz eventually learned that they had lost their parents, their little brother, their home, and all traces of their childhood. They had to go forward into the future completely on their own.

How do you think Benno and Heinz were able to deal with their loss? What gave them the strength to carry on and rebuild their lives?

7. During the war, many people were bystanders to brutal atrocities, while others found the courage to protest, as well as to help and hide the victims, most of whom were strangers.

It takes courage to stand up to injustice. Why do some individuals and groups help others in times of crisis, while others turn away?

Do you think you could put yourself or your family in danger to help a total stranger?

8. Over 1,000,000 Canadian men and women fought bravely with the Allies during World War II, with more than 45,000 losing their lives in the global struggle to end Nazi domination. In spite of their efforts, at the end of the war the world learnt the extent of Hitler's "Final Solution": 6,000,000 Jews had been murdered in the Holocaust, including 1,500,000 Jewish children.

What unique lessons can we learn from the Holocaust?

After the war, the rallying cry was "Never Again". Can you think of places in the world where mass slaughter is being committed even today, and children are the victims of conflict? What could the rest of the world do for these children?

9. The Canadian approach to multiculturalism is acceptance of all people, regardless of where they come from, what they look like and what religion they follow. Official Canadian policy values these differences and embraces the rich diversity of all ethnic, cultural, religious and linguistic groups.

Are Canadians truly respectful of the differences of others? How can we educate people to be more tolerant?

10. Here in Canada, neo-Nazis continue to glorify Hitler and his regime, and deny the fact of the Holocaust. Their hate propaganda has contributed to an increase in anti-Semitism, as documented in the League for Human Rights' annual *Audit of Antisemitic Incidents*. This study documented 935 hate-related incidents against Jews in Canada in 2006 alone, including physical assaults, damage to synagogues and cemeteries, and messages of hate over the Internet.

What can we do as individuals and as a society to stop intolerance and hatred before it leads to brutality and even genocide?

OUR FAMILY

Grandparents
Frumke   1880–1947

Parents
Max   1898–1943
Golda   1905–1943

The Boys   **The Wives**
Heinz   1925–1988   Fella   1925–
Benno   1929–   Rita   1930–
Charlie   1936–1943

Heinz's Children   **The Spouses**
Danny   1950–1977
Ann   1957–   Michael   1950–
David   1960–   Sharon   1964–

Heinz's Grandchildren
Jason   1988–
Toni   1991–
Victoria   1992–
Joel   1992–
Dana   1994–
Charlie   1997–

Benno's Girls   **The Husbands**
Susy   1955–   Brian   1955–
Gina   1957–   Graeme   1954–
Wendy   1961–   David   1959–

Benno's Grandchildren
Laura   1984–
Julie   1986–
Samantha   1986–
Jeffrey   1988–
Zoe   1989–
Max   1989–
Emilie   1992–